The Brothers Grimm Spectaculathon

(one-act)

A SHORT COMEDY BY

Don Zolidis

The Brothers Grimm Spectaculathon (one-act) - 2021 edition.
Copyright © 2007 Don Zolidis. ALL RIGHTS RESERVED

The Rules in Brief

- DO NOT perform this Play without obtaining prior permission from Playscripts, and without paying the required royalty.

- DO NOT photocopy, scan, or otherwise duplicate any part of this book.

- DO NOT alter the text of the Play, change a character's gender, delete any dialogue, cut any music, or alter any objectionable language, unless explicitly authorized by Playscripts.

- DO provide the required credit to the author(s) and the required attribution to Playscripts in all programs and promotional literature associated with any performance of this Play.

Copyright Basics

This Play is protected by United States and international copyright law. These laws ensure that authors are rewarded for creating new and vital dramatic work, and protect them against theft and abuse of their work.

A play is a piece of property, fully owned by the author, just like a house or car. You must obtain permission to use this property, and must pay a royalty fee for the privilege—whether or not you charge an admission fee. Playscripts collects these required payments on behalf of the author.

Anyone who violates an author's copyright is liable as a copyright infringer under United States and international law. Playscripts and the author are entitled to institute legal action for any such infringement, which can subject the infringer to actual damages, statutory damages, and attorneys' fees. A court may impose statutory damages of up to $150,000 for willful copyright infringements. U.S. copyright law also provides for possible criminal sanctions. Visit the website of the U.S. Copyright Office (www.copyright.gov) for more information.

THE BOTTOM LINE: If you break copyright law, you are robbing a playwright and opening yourself to expensive legal action. Follow the rules, and when in doubt, ask us.

Cast of Characters

NARRATOR 1 *(female — maybe)*
NARRATOR 2 *(male — maybe)*
ACTOR
GIRL
DIRT MERCHANT
RUMPELSTILTSKIN
ENCHANTRESS
THE DEVIL
PRINCE
RAPUNZEL
AUDIENCE MEMBER
HANSEL
GRETEL
WITCH
DWARF 1
DWARF 2
SNOW WHITE
WITCH 2
PRINCE 2
JOHANNES
RAVEN
KING
QUEEN
PLINKIE PLIE
CINDERELLA

How To Cast This Show

Smallest cast: This play could be done with a total of 5 actors. With a small cast, the narrators become characters in the scenes as indicated. Everyone should have lots of costumes available.

Largest cast: Every role is played by a different actor. Different narrators may play the narrator roles in each fairy tale.

Casting Notes

Any of the roles may be played by any actor of any gender, race, or ethnicity. There are some moments, when actors switch roles, that it might be funnier if Dwarf 2 was played by a male-presenting person and Snow White was played by a female-presenting person, but in general there's no reason to be overly restrictive in casting. This is all make-believe here.

Running Time

Speed is of the essence with this show. Keep scene changes absolutely minimal. The one-act version of this play runs about 1 hour, maybe a little longer. If you need to make it shorter, feel free to make any cuts necessary for time. You can also remove an entire fairy tale (Hansel and Gretel or Snow White or Faithful Johannes) if you need to. Feel free to adjust lines as necessary to make it make sense.

Author's Note

It has been nearly fifteen years since I wrote the original *Brothers Grimm Spectaculathon*. With over 3,000 productions worldwide, it's been my most popular show by a long ways. Returning to an old play is always a crapshoot—there's always the risk of ruining something. There are things I would change, better jokes, but sometimes removing the warts from something doesn't make it turn into a prince, it makes it turn into a less interesting frog.

I am not the playwright I was fifteen years ago. I hope I'm a better one, but the results will be in the execution, not in me merely wishing it to be so. The original *BGS* has a madcap, free-wheeling, almost dangerous energy to it. The play feels like it could run off the rails at any time, and only the efforts of a talented group of actors are keeping this unwieldy massive thing moving forward. That's probably part of the reason actors and audiences enjoy doing it so much: you never know what's going to happen next.

The last thing I want to do is make this play safe. But I'd like to make it safe for the actors to perform.

THE BROTHERS GRIMM SPECTACULATHON

(ONE-ACT VERSION)

by Don Zolidis

(The stage can be anything, really.)

(NARRATOR 1 enters.)

NARRATOR 1. Hello and welcome to the Brothers Grimm Spectaculathon.

(NARRATOR 2 bursts onto the stage.)

NARRATOR 2. SUNDAY SUNDAY SUNDAY! It's EXTREME! See! Monster slaying action as the three-headed pig battles the wolf-o-bot in a bone-crushing cage match of death! They'll huff and they'll puff and they'll kick some iron! Aaaaaaaaah!

(Short pause. NARRATOR 1 blinks.)

NARRATOR 1. What we are going to do here today—

NARRATOR 2. And then the battle you've been waiting for: Snow White vs. Sleeping Beauty in a mud-wrestling death match. Who's the toughest of them all?!

NARRATOR 1. Can you stop please?

NARRATOR 2. We've got unhinged princess action! Elsa and Rapunzel in a hair-pulling smackdown! Let go! Let IT GOOOOO!

NARRATOR 1. Okay, stop. We're not doing that.

(NARRATOR 2 ignites a Firestarter.)

NARRATOR 2. Flames! Flames!

NARRATOR 1. *[Actor's name].* You're doing it again. What did we talk about?

NARRATOR 2. About not being awesome?

NARRATOR 1. This—is the Brothers Grimm Spectaculathon!

NARRATOR 2. That's right. And what we are about to do today is going to blow your mind. You will never be the same. Forget your marriage. Forget your children. If you haven't already.

NARRATOR 1. If you need to go to the bathroom, we'll wait. We don't want accidents.

(NARRATOR 2 *points to someone in the audience.*)

NARRATOR 2. You look a little touch-and-go miss. Are you sure? You okay? All right then.

(To the other NARRATOR.*)*

Keep an eye on that one.

NARRATOR 1. A little background to begin:

NARRATOR 2. The Brothers Grimm were brothers named Grimm. They are dead. But in the period before they died the Brothers Grimm wrote 209 fairy tales that we know today—

NARRATOR 1. They didn't write them.

NARRATOR 2. The Brothers Grimm did not write 209 fairy tales that we know today, they were frauds. We should dig up their bodies and spit on their corpses.

NARRATOR 1. No I'm just saying they were collectors of stories.

NARRATOR 2. Never mind that last part.

NARRATOR 1. And these stories have become extremely popular. We all know them today:

NARRATOR 2. Such stories as The Wolf and the Seven Young Kids—

NARRATOR 1. The Pack of Ragamuffins—

NARRATOR 2. And Straw, Coal, and Bean.

NARRATOR 1. I forgot about that one.

NARRATOR 2. Oh yeah. Straw, Coal, and Bean? Only the best fairy tale in the entire history of the world. I'm literally like crying buckets by the end of it. Changed my life. I can't even look at straw, coal, or beans anymore.

NARRATOR 1. What's it about?

NARRATOR 2. No idea.

NARRATOR 1. Those might not be household names, but quite a few of these stories have become immortalized in film and television—

NARRATOR 2. Of course they've all been changed by "the mouse"—

(He lifts a sign into view that says "Disney".)

—to feed their enormous octopus-like animation empire which sucks the life out of existence and crushes your soul in a death-grip of happy happy songs and talking objects. I can't even speak their name aloud because they're for a way to sue me right now.

(He swings a lightsaber.)

NARRATOR 2. You'll never take me alive, Imagineers!

NARRATOR 1. You know they own Star Wars too.

NARRATOR 2. *(Dropping lightsaber:)* Ah! They're everywhere!

NARRATOR 1. O-kay. What we are going to do for you right now is return these fairy tales to their original glory. We have assembled the greatest troupe of actors the world has even seen and—

(ACTOR enters, scratching themselves.)

ACTOR. I thought there was supposed to be catering back here?

NARRATOR 2. There's like a beef thing somewhere.

ACTOR. Where?

NARRATOR 2. I don't know—in the back somewhere.

ACTOR. Is there anything to drink?

NARRATOR 2. No.

(ACTOR exits, annoyed.)

NARRATOR 1. These actors are so insanely talented that—

ACTOR. *(Offstage:)* I don't see it!

NARRATOR 2. Do you see the radiator?

ACTOR. *(Offstage:)* No! Oh wait! No.

NARRATOR 2. There's probably someone sitting on it. Move them.

ACTOR. *(Offstage:)* Oh here it is.

ANOTHER ACTOR. *(Offstage:)* Hey!

NARRATOR 1. Anyway, in the short time we have, our crack team of actors is going to perform all 209 fairy tales of the Brothers Grimm.

NARRATOR 2. That's like three stories per minute.

NARRATOR 1. Or a different number if you know math. And we're going to keep the original endings intact!

NARRATOR 2. Blood! Violence! Death! People being cut open with scissors!

NARRATOR 1. *And* to make things more difficult, we're going to perform them as originally intended, which is . . .

NARRATOR 2. That it's all one giant super mega-juicy story.

NARRATOR 1. Are you ready?!

NARRATOR 2. I'm so excited I'm going to throw up. Does anyone have a hat? Nope? Excuse me then.

(NARRATOR 2 *exits.* NARRATOR 1 *stretches and does warm-ups. Perhaps a few wind sprints.*)

NARRATOR 1. Well I don't know when he'll be back—

(*We hear sounds of him vomiting offstage.*)

So . . . Once upon a time . . .

(GIRL *enters.*)

There was a girl who was raised by wolves and whose mother died in childbirth and she was abandoned by her father who could spin straw into a gold and made a deal with a series of elves if they would help him make shoes. There was also a talking fox in there somewhere.

NARRATOR 2. (*Returning:*) And she was beautiful—

NARRATOR 1. Because no one cares about ugly people.

NARRATOR 2. Whoa.

NARRATOR 1. Point me to an ugly Disney princess.

NARRATOR 2. Snow White.

NARRATOR 1. Literally the fairest of them all.

NARRATOR 2. Not my thing, sorry. She's got that whiny voice.

NARRATOR 1. Anyway, there was a girl.

NARRATOR 2. And she was poor.

GIRL. Oh I am poor.

NARRATOR 2. Dirt poor.

NARRATOR 1. She couldn't even afford dirt.

(DIRT MERCHANT *enters.*)

DIRT MERCHANT. Dirt for sale! Dirt for sale! Hey, you! Get off the merchandise!

(*He exits.*)

GIRL. (*Crying:*) I shall flood the ground with my tears!

(DIRT MERCHANT *returns.*)

DIRT MERCHANT. You're getting it wet! Stop it!

(*He exits.*)

GIRL. If only I could live in a boot or make some deals with elves or find a talking fox.

(An ENCHANTRESS *[played by* NARRATOR 1*] enters.)*

ENCHANTRESS. Excuse me—but I couldn't help overhearing your tale of misery and woe. Tell you what—I will grant you your heart's desire if you give me one small thing.

GIRL. That sounds like a great bargain. I won't even ask what the small thing is because I'm so trusting!

ENCHANTRESS. Excellent. *(She makes a magical signal.)* I vanish.

(She does not actually appear to vanish. ENCHANTRESS *looks around and covers* GIRL's *eyes.)*

ENCHANTRESS. I vanish again.

(She quickly hides behind something.)

GIRL. What a nice lady.

*(*THE DEVIL *[played by* NARRATOR 2*] enters.)*

THE DEVIL. Hey there hot stuff. Oh wait, that's me. Ha ha ha ha!

GIRL. Are you a prince?

THE DEVIL. Of darkness.

(He laughs at his own joke.)

Oh that's clever! Now, I happened to overhear your tale of misery and woe and I'm here to help.

GIRL. Well actually I just —

THE DEVIL. *(Handing her a contract:)* Just sign this one small contract and you shall conceive a daughter so beautiful she will be selected to be in a game show with 22 other attractive women competing for the love of—

GIRL. Done.

(She signs the contract.)

THE DEVIL. Moo ah ha ha ha ha ha!

(He looks around. Then runs off.)

GIRL. This is a busy street.

*(*RUMPELSTILTSKIN *enters, limping and grotesque.)*

RUMPELSTILTSKIN. Hello there.

GIRL. You're hideous and deformed!

RUMPELSTILTSKIN. That's hurtful, but I have a great bargain for—

GIRL. My stomach recoils in horror as you approach!

RUMPELSTILTSKIN. Do you want to hear my offer or not?

GIRL. Sure. Go ahead. You're probably trustworthy and I'm stupid and don't judge people by their appearances.

RUMPELSTILTSKIN. I shall make you rich, rich I tell you! Beyond your wildest dreams!

GIRL. Really? Because I have some pretty wild dreams.

(She takes out a notebook labeled "MY WILD DREAMS"— hands it over—)

(RUMPELSTILTSKIN opens it up, recoils.)

RUMPELSTILTSKIN. This is really messed up. You seriously need help. A lot of work has gone into this and it's disturbing.

GIRL. I also want a jet fighter with Tom Cruise in it—when he was 23 and not into the weird stuff.

RUMPELSTILTSKIN. He was still into that. He just wasn't advertising.

GIRL. I want a Tom Cruise clone then. That I control.

RUMPELSTILTSKIN. I shall make you rich. Not rich enough to afford a jet fighter or to steal a skin graft from a famous actor and grow a clone in a vat, but rich enough! And I ask only one small thing in return.

GIRL. Sounds good.

RUMPELSTILTSKIN. Don't you want to know what the small thing is?

GIRL. No I'm cool.

RUMPELSTILTSKIN. Very well!

(He snickers and exits.)

(NARRATOR 1 re-emerges.)

NARRATOR 1. It was a good day for the girl. She fell in love with a prince.

(PRINCE [possibly played by NARRATOR 2] enters.)

PRINCE. Hey you're hot.

GIRL. So are you!

PRINCE. Let's get married!

GIRL. Score!

(*They air kiss.*)

NARRATOR 1. She grew very rich.

PRINCE. Hey look I just tripped over a giant pot of gold! What are the odds!

GIRL. Ha ha! Score!

NARRATOR 1. And she conceived a child.

(*PRINCE looks confused. GIRL looks sheepish.*)

PRINCE. Whoa. How did that happen?

GIRL. Um . . .

NARRATOR 2. You see kids, when a prince and princess love each other very much —

NARRATOR 1. Through magic! Magic of the Devil! And that's where babies come from.

(*NARRATOR 2 goes back to being the PRINCE.*)

PRINCE. I've always wanted a baby. Let's go back to my kingdom.

(*PRINCE and GIRL hop forward. GIRL [possibly] puts a pillow under her shirt.*)

GIRL. It's terrible here.

PRINCE. Ha ha yes.

GIRL. Ah! The baby's coming!

PRINCE. Dang it! I mean—push or breathe or something!

GIRL. You're not helping!

PRINCE. I'm not trying to! You can do it! I'm gonna be over here!

NARRATOR 1. The miracle of childbirth.

GIRL. I hate you I hate you I hate you I hate you

PRINCE. Focus your anger! Focus your anger!

(*GIRL screams.*)

GIRL. Aaaaaaaah!

PRINCE. Aaaaaaaah!

(*GIRL screams. Nothing happens. She screams again.*)

PRINCE. I can see her little head!

(GIRL *screams again. A baby doll is thrown in from offstage.* PRINCE *snatches it out of the air like a Frisbee.*)

PRINCE. Oh it's so beautiful!

NARRATOR 2. Years passed.

(The PRINCE *throws the baby offstage like a Frisbee.)*

And she grew into a beautiful young teenager, Rapunzel.

PRINCE. I want to revisit the name Rapunzel. What about Amber?

GIRL. That was the name of your ex-girlfriend!

PRINCE. AMBER WAS NICE TO ME!

*(*RAPUNZEL *enters, wearing headphones and ignoring everyone.)*

PRINCE. Are you going to wear your hair like that?

RAPUNZEL. Shut up.

GIRL. Honey, we're going to have dinner so wash your hands.

RAPUNZEL. You can't tell me what to do.

PRINCE. Don't talk to your mother that way. She sold her soul to the Devil just to have you—

RAPUNZEL. I don't care. I didn't ask to be born! I'm going out.

GIRL. You're not walking out of this house, young lady!

RAPUNZEL. I do what I want. You don't know me.

PRINCE. I've had just about enough of this "parenting"! I'm going golfing.

*(*PRINCE *exits.)*

RAPUNZEL. Real winner you chose there, Mom.

GIRL. You don't have a lot of time to be choosy when you fall in love at first sight.

NARRATOR 1. And just then . . .

*(*NARRATOR 1 *switches back to the* ENCHANTRESS.)*

ENCHANTRESS. I have returned.

*(THE DEVIL *pops in.)*

THE DEVIL. Your time is up.

*(*RUMPELSTILTSKIN *returns.)*

RUMPELSTILTSKIN. You know I was in the neighborhood and I was thinking that I forgot something like eighteen years ago, and then I was like, oh yeah, I was supposed to get that thing from that girl. And then here I was, right at your house?

GIRL. What do you want?

ALL THREE. Your child!

> *(They all start arguing amongst themselves.)*
> *(GIRL takes RAPUNZEL aside.)*

RAPUNZEL. Mom?!

GIRL. What.

RAPUNZEL. How many deals did you make?

GIRL. Just three. And I may have promised your hand in marriage to a talking rabbit. What? I was young, I needed the money—and the baby—and the prince—but mostly just the money and the baby.

RAPUNZEL. This is why I'm in therapy!

GIRL. Oh honey you're not in therapy because of my deals, you're in therapy because we're terrible parents.

THE DEVIL. You heard what I said—witch.

ENCHANTRESS. For the last time, I'm an Enchantress!

RUMPELSTILTSKIN. Girl, if you can guess my name, I will release you from our bargain.

THE DEVIL. It's Rumpelstiltskin.

GIRL. Rumpelstiltskin.

> *(ENCHANTRESS becomes NARRATOR 1 for a moment.)*

NARRATOR 1. And the little man stomped his feet so hard they broke through the floor, and when tried to pull them out, he broke in half.

RUMPELSTILTSKIN. Seriously? That's how I die? I get my foot caught and break in half trying to get it out?

NARRATOR 1. Yep.

THE DEVIL. *(Pointing:)* Ha ha.

RUMPELSTILTSKIN. That's gotta be the stupidest way to die ever.

> *(RUMPELSTILTSKIN breaks himself in half.)*

RUMPELSTILTSKIN. Aaaagghh!

> *(NARRATOR 1 jumps back into being the ENCHANTRESS.)*

RAPUNZEL. I'm not cleaning that up.

ENCHANTRESS. Now that that horrid little man is gone, I will take Rapunzel.

(She grabs one of RAPUNZEL's arms.)

THE DEVIL. Um . . . excuse me? I'm the Devil.

(He grabs her other arm.)

I've got more claim than some stupid little witch.

ENCHANTRESS. Enchantress!

THE DEVIL. Whatever. Witch.

ENCHANTRESS. That's it! Let's go!

(She drops RAPUNZEL's arm and takes out a wand.)

THE DEVIL. Oh you want some, huh?

(He starts feinting towards her.)

RAPUNZEL. Mom, let's get out of here!

GIRL. Quiet honey I'm watching this. Go Devil!

(She takes out a Duke or Arizona State [or just a sign that says "Go Devil"] pennant and starts waving it.)

ENCHANTRESS. Expelliarmus!

THE DEVIL. That's a witch spell!

ENCHANTRESS. Fine I curse you!

THE DEVIL. You know what, this is stupid. Tell ya what, if you sign this contract here, I will let you take Rapunzel.

(He takes out a contract. It says "EVIL CONTRACT WITH THE DEVIL.")

ENCHANTRESS. Oh this seems legit.

(She signs it.)

THE DEVIL. Moo ah ha ha! And I disappear in a cloud of brimstone!

(He slowly disappears making weird motions with his hands. Returns momentarily as NARRATOR 2.)

ENCHANTRESS. Well, come along Rapunzel.

RAPUNZEL. Where are we going?

ENCHANTRESS. I've got this great tower for you.

GIRL. Run along dear.

RAPUNZEL. But Mom, I don't want to go with the evil Enchantress.

GIRL. Yeah I didn't want to raise a spoiled brat, but sometimes you don't get what you want. Unless you make a deal with the Devil and some other weird people. See ya.

(RAPUNZEL *exits with the* ENCHANTRESS.)

NARRATOR 2. So the Enchantress took Rapunzel and locked her in a high tower without stairs or door. As for the Girl and her Prince—

(PRINCE *returns.*)

PRINCE. I'm back from my golf trip. What did I miss?

GIRL. The forces of darkness battled it out for our daughter's soul.

PRINCE. Cool. You want to go to Hawaii?

GIRL. Rock on.

(*They skip offstage.*)

NARRATOR 2. And they lived happily ever after.

NARRATOR 1. But our story is not even remotely finished.

NARRATOR 2. No wait, it is finished. It's not yet begun.

NARRATOR 1. That's right.

NARRATOR 2. So let's go back to that girl—Rapunzel's mother.

NARRATOR 1. You might be familiar with her mother.

(GRETEL *enters.*)

(NARRATOR 2 *becomes* HANSEL.)

(*Both* GRETEL *and* HANSEL *speak with exaggerated German accents.*)

HANSEL. Gretel! What are you doing out?!

GRETEL. Nothing.

HANSEL. You seem moody lately. As if something were bothering you.

GRETEL. Ya . . . It's . . . our mother. You see, our mother died before we were born.

HANSEL. I remember.

NARRATOR 1. Our next story: Hansel. And. Gretel. Or: The original horror movie.

GRETEL. I'm haunted Hansel. Haunted by her memory.

HANSEL. Ya I too am haunted. Perhaps we ought to go into the woods where it's dark and scary.

NARRATOR 1. Can we get some cool lighting effects please?

(A cool lighting effect happens. NARRATOR 1 *addresses part of the audience.)*

NARRATOR 1. Okay. Now I need your help. You people over here— Awake? Good. Here's what we're going to do. When I point to you I want you to make a scary horror movie music sound like this.

(Imitating the sound of a well-known horror movie:)

Ch-ch-ch-ch-ch. A-a-a-a-a-a. Ch-ch-ch-ch-ch. A-a-a-a-a-a. Can we try that?

(The audience tries it. NARRATOR 1 *ad-libs a reaction such as: "You suck," "What horror movies have you been watching?" "This guy isn't scary," etc. He may make them try again as needed before moving to another section of the audience.)*

NARRATOR 1. Now, you guys. You look a little smarter than those people over there. I'm sorry, it's true. Look at this guy over here. He's a freaking genius. Right? He's a freaking genius. Now—when I point to you, I want you to say, "Don't go in there!" Okay, let's try that. One. Two Three.

(The audience says, "Don't go in there!" NARRATOR 1 *ad-libs reaction before moving to a third section.)*

NARRATOR 1. Now you guys. No good horror movie is complete without heavy breathing. Like this:

(He does heavy breathing.)

You try it.

(Points to a couple in the audience.)

Um . . . you need to take it outside, okay? This is a family show.

(He addresses the entire audience.)

All right? Everybody got it?! One last test.

(He points at each group in turn very quickly.)

And back with our story.

GRETEL. Hansel, I am worried.

HANSEL. Why?

GRETEL. I overheard our wicked stepmother saying she was going to take us into the woods and leave us to be eaten by wolves.

HANSEL. Ya she does that.

GRETEL. I say we go into the woods ourselves.

(NARRATOR 1 *points to the audience.*)

AUDIENCE. DON'T GO IN THERE!

HANSEL. Okay, let's go.

(*They hop forward.*)

(*Perhaps the lights change again. Maybe they have flashlights now.*)

GRETEL. Here we are in the dark and scary woods alone.

(NARRATOR *points to one group.*)

AUDIENCE. Ch-ch-ch-ch. A-a-a-a. Ch-ch-ch-ch. A-a-a-a.

GRETEL. Something's not right

HANSEL. You're just a chicken.

GRETEL. I feel so strange, Hansel. What's that?!

(NARRATOR 1 *points again.*)

AUDIENCE. Ch-ch-ch-ch. A-a-a-a. Ch-ch-ch-ch. A-a-a-a.

HANSEL. Looks like a house.

GRETEL. It's made out of candy.

HANSEL. This isn't suspicious at all.

GRETEL. Do you want to try the door?

(HANSEL *moves forward.*)

(NARRATOR 1 *points again.*)

AUDIENCE. DON'T GO IN THERE!

HANSEL. Do you think I should? If only I had some kind of clue about what to do.

(NARRATOR 1 *points again.*)

AUDIENCE. DON'T GO IN THERE!

HANSEL. Huh. Let's go in there.

(NARRATOR 1 *makes a sound effect like a door creaking open.*)

GRETEL. It's dark in here.

(NARRATOR 1 *points to a group.*)

AUDIENCE. Ch-ch-ch-ch. A-a-a-a-a. Ch-ch-ch-ch. A-a-a-a-a.

(NARRATOR 1 *points to the other group.*)

AUDIENCE. (*Heavy breathing.*)

GRETEL. Is that your hand?

(NARRATOR1 *points again.*)

AUDIENCE. *(Heavy breathing.)*

HANSEL. Is that . . . your hand?

(NARRATOR 1 *points again.*)

AUDIENCE. Ch-ch-ch-ch. A-a-a-a-a. Ch-ch-ch-ch. A-a-a-a-a.

(WITCH *enters, sneaking up behind them.*)

(*An* AUDIENCE MEMBER *[a plant] in the front row munching on popcorn, freaks out—would be great if this were an adult.*)

AUDIENCE MEMBER. She's behind you! Look behind you! Turn around!

(AUDIENCE MEMBER *stands up and screams, pointing at the* WITCH.)

AUDIENCE MEMBER. TURN AROUND LOOK BEHIND YOU THERE'S A WITCH BEHIND YOU! SHE'S RIGHT THERE! SHE'S RIGHT THERE!

WITCH. Are you eating my house?

HANSEL and GRETEL. Aaaaaaah!

AUDIENCE MEMBER. I TOLD YOU! I TOLD YOU BUT YOU DIDN'T LISTEN! WHY DIDN'T YOU LISTEN TO ME?! I SAID "DON'T GO IN THERE" AND YOU WENT IN! YOU WENT IN! WHYYYYY?!

NARRATOR 1. Sir?

AUDIENCE MEMBER. What?

NARRATOR 1. Can we keep doing the play please?

AUDIENCE MEMBER. You said it was a horror movie so—

NARRATOR 1. Let's take it down a notch, all right?

(AUDIENCE MEMBER *sits back down.*)

AUDIENCE MEMBER. My bad, my bad.

GRETEL. Were you eating the house, Hansel?

HANSEL. Maybe? I was hungry. It was made of candy! You should try the floorboards, they're really tasty.

WITCH. I'm so disappointed in today's young people. You think you can build a house out of candy and no one's going to disturb it, but noooo . . . I'm going to have to teach you a lesson.

AUDIENCE MEMBER. OH DANG IT! I KNEW IT! GET OUT! GET OUT OF THE HOUSE!

GRETEL. What kind of lesson?

AUDIENCE MEMBER. SHE'S GONNA EAT YOU! WHY ARE YOU TALKING TO HER?! RUN!

WITCH. But first, why don't you want more candy?

AUDIENCE MEMBER. NO! SHE'S JUST FATTENING YOU UP! THAT'S ALL SHE'S DOING!

NARRATOR 1. So Hansel and Gretel stayed with the witch and ate and ate—

(AUDIENCE MEMBER *stomps around and throws things, protesting.*)

AUDIENCE MEMBER. DUMB!

NARRATOR 1. And they got fatter and fatter—and the witch was very nice to them.

HANSEL. Why does my cologne smell like gravy?

(AUDIENCE MEMBER *raises their hand vigorously.*)

GRETEL. Look, she gave me this apple to put in my mouth? Wasn't that nice?

(GRETEL *puts the apple in her mouth.*)

AUDIENCE MEMBER. OH COME ON!

WITCH. Well, my children, I am just an old woman in the woods—

AUDIENCE MEMBER. NO SHE AIN'T! I'VE GOT THE PROGRAM RIGHT HERE!

WITCH. And I could use some help.

HANSEL. What is it?

WITCH. I need some help cleaning out . . . my oven.

AUDIENCE MEMBER. OH HECK NO! NOOO! DON'T DO IT!

HANSEL. Oh I can help with that.

(NARRATOR 1 *points to the audience group.*)

AUDIENCE. DON'T GO IN THERE!

AUDIENCE MEMBER. I DON'T EVEN KNOW WHY WE HAVE TO TELL YOU!

WITCH. Come along, Hamsel.

HANSEL. It's Hansel.

WITCH. Oh right. Hansel.

(She chuckles evilly.)

AUDIENCE MEMBER. OHHHH I CAN'T WATCH!

GRETEL. Oh. Hey. I dropped a quarter. Can you pick it up?

WITCH. A quarter?

(She bends down.)

GRETEL. Eat this, witch!

(GRETEL *makes a shoving motion towards the* WITCH.)

WITCH. Aaaaaaaah!

AUDIENCE MEMBER. YESSSS! WOOO! YESSS! YESS!

HANSEL. You did it.

AUDIENCE MEMBER. Wait a minute. She ain't dead. This is where they get you. Don't let your guard down.

GRETEL. Yes, it is all happy now.

AUDIENCE MEMBER. No it isn't! She's coming back! I've seen this movie!

HANSEL. How about we eat the rest of the house?

GRETEL. Good idea.

(They start snacking. WITCH *rises up.)*

AUDIENCE MEMBER. NO I SEE HER! SHE'S BEHIND YOU AGAIN YOU IDIOTS!

(GRETEL *turns and shoves her back in.)*

WITCH. I'm melting! Oh wait . . . I'm burning!

(She dies.)

HANSEL. Ding dong the witch is dead!

NARRATOR 1. Wrong story.

HANSEL. I get so confused.

NARRATOR 1. So they made it. But the horror wasn't over. Because early childhood trauma can affect a lot of fairytale heroes. And Hansel . . . well . . . let's just say he developed a problem.

HANSEL. Gretel, you want to try fairy dust?

GRETEL. No, Hansel. You have a problem and you need help.

HANSEL. It lets you fly.

GRETEL. It doesn't let you fly, Hansel. Drugs are bad.

HANSEL. These are natural. From ground-up fairies. Let me show you.

NARRATOR 1. And he jumped off a cliff.

HANSEL. I can fly! Maybe.

NARRATOR 1. It's up to you, audience. If you clap hard enough, Hansel will live. Come on people!

HANSEL. *(Imploring the audience:)* Come on people! Let me live!

NARRATOR 1. Come on! Don't you believe a boy can fly?!?! Come on!

(A light begins to shine on HANSEL, growing brighter.)

Come on you can do it!

(The light and noise crescendo.)

HANSEL. *(Desperate:)* Come on out there! Please!

(The light suddenly goes out.)

Aaaaaaaah.

(HANSEL makes a "splat!" noise.)

(Pause. NARRATOR 1 looks sad.)

NARRATOR 1. You didn't clap hard enough. He died. You know I've . . . done this show a lot. And every time the audience clapped hard enough to let Hansel live. Every time. I just don't know what to say.

(NARRATOR 1 picks someone in the audience.)

I think really it comes down to this guy. This guy right here. He didn't clap hard enough. His heart wasn't really into it. How do you face your children, sir? How do you face your children?

(If the audience member is about to respond.)

Don't talk to me.

GRETEL. Hansel?

NARRATOR 1. He's in a better place now, Gretel. Where his stupidity can't hurt him anymore.

GRETEL. Canada?

NARRATOR 1. If you want it to be Canada.

NARRATOR 1. *(Suddenly chipper again:)* Anyway, after Hansel's untimely death, thank you very much Mr. *[describes audience member],* she married a wandering woodcutter. And they had a daughter. Who would grow up to make a deal with several supernatural entities who would eventually imprison her daughter in the tower.

(NARRATOR 2 *returns.)*

NARRATOR 2. But.

NARRATOR 1. There's always a but.

NARRATOR 2. One question remains:

NARRATOR 1. Where did the witch come from?

NARRATOR 2. Ooh I know. Once upon a time. There was a dwarf.

(DWARF 1 *enters.)*

DWARF 1. I prefer little person.

NARRATOR 1. In fact, two dwarves.

(DWARF 2 *[played by* NARRATOR 2] *enters.)*

DWARF 2. I prefer dwarf.

NARRATOR 1. And these dwarves worked all day in the mines.

DWARF 1. *(Singing:)* I've been workin' on the railroad—

NARRATOR 1. Mines!

DWARF 2. *(Singing:)* Whistle while you work

NARRATOR 1. We can't use that song.

DWARF 2. I do what I want.

NARRATOR 1. No it's like copyrighted, we can't use it. The Mouse will sue us. So the dwarves worked in the mines, they sang their little song, and then one day they came home to find—

(SNOW WHITE *enters. She whines petulantly and falls asleep.)*

DWARF 1. What the heck is that thing?

DWARF 2. She's huge! Get her away from me! She's going to eat me!

(DWARF 2 *dives and hides.)*

NARRATOR 1. You see, in those days, most people were cannibals. Which explains the witch from before. The first Dwarf, though, who we will name . . . Slappy, wasn't afraid.

DWARF 1. Gar. I like ladies. So . . . uh . . . baby, I couldn't help noticing that you're in my bed—

(He moves towards her.)

NARRATOR 1. Whoa! This is a children's story.

DWARF 1. So I'm going to chop you up and eat you.

(DWARF 1 takes out a fork and knife.)

NARRATOR 1. Time out. Time out. Put away the hot sauce.

(DWARF 1 hides a bottle of hot sauce behind his back.)

DWARF 1. What? I'm just going with what my character wants.

NARRATOR 1. You do not get to eat Snow White. You're not the villain of the story.

DWARF 1. No. Look. I've been doing some character work. Slappy has had a hard life. He's been discriminated against for being a dwarf. And he hates the world. He just hates it—

NARRATOR 1. He does not!

DWARF 1. And he wants revenge against the humans who have wronged him, so when this giant chick comes into his home and sleeps in his bed . . . dinner time.

(NARRATOR 2 enters.)

NARRATOR 1. No. We are going to do this story as written! Snow White cleans house for the seven dwarves, then she gets poisoned by an apple, then a prince shows up and falls in love with her because she's unconscious and can't talk back.

NARRATOR 2. You know, maybe this fairy tale is a little antiquated.

NARRATOR 1. This is a classic. What girl out there didn't want to be a house maid to seven freaky bearded dudes and then have no choice in who she was going to marry?

NARRATOR 2. Sometimes the classics are . . . how do you say, bad?

NARRATOR 1. They're beautiful!

NARRATOR 2. Really? Let me show you one.

(NARRATOR 2 takes out the big book of fairy tales.)

Here we go—number 191. Lean Lisa.

NARRATOR 1. Never heard of it.

(SNOW WHITE wakes up.)

SNOW WHITE. Question: Why is it that I have to clean and cook for the dwarves? If I'm a princess, shouldn't they be cooking and cleaning for me?

NARRATOR 2. Both of you stop, okay? We're doing a new one, Lean Lisa.

SNOW WHITE. Never heard of it.

NARRATOR 2. So once upon a time, Lean Lisa lay in bed with her husband, Long Laurence.

DWARF 1. Do I get to be Long Laurence?

NARRATOR 2. Yes.

DWARF 1. Sweet.

(DWARF 1 *and* SNOW WHITE *rearrange themselves.*)

SNOW WHITE. Dear husband, I was thinking.

DWARF 1. I'm trying to sleep, woman.

SNOW WHITE. I'm tired of being poor and hungry. What if we took the cow in the field and tried to get her to have calves? Then we could raise the calves and sell them and we'd have enough money to buy more animals. And then we wouldn't have to starve any more.

DWARF 1. That sounds like a lot of work.

SNOW WHITE. You're lazy!

DWARF 1. Quiet your wagging tongue woman!

(DWARF 1 *strangles* SNOW WHITE.)

NARRATOR 2. And she died. The end.

(SNOW WHITE *falls over. The end.*)

NARRATOR 1. Seriously? That's what it says?

NARRATOR 2. Right here.

NARRATOR 1. Wow. That story's awful.

(SNOW WHITE *wakes up again.*)

SNOW WHITE. Can I go back to being Sleeping Beauty now?

NARRATOR 2. I thought you were supposed to be Snow White.

SNOW WHITE. Can anyone really tell the difference? Seriously, they're the same story.

NARRATOR 2. Anyway, what I'm saying is that these stories need some spicing up here and there. A new angle. A new way of putting them together.

NARRATOR 1. Fine. I don't care anymore. Whatever. I'm sure this Dwarf is going to do a better job than me. Go ahead take my place.

(DWARF 1 jumps up.)

DWARF 1. Sounds good.

NARRATOR 1. Wait, I didn't—

DWARF 1. All right, you're gonna be Dwarf 1, all right?

(NARRATOR 1 puts on a beard.)

DWARF 1. *[Narrator 2 actor's name].* You're Dwarf 2. I'm the new narrator.

SNOW WHITE. Am I still Snow White?

DWARF 1. You're whatever you want to be honey. Call me. So, once upon a time there was a house filled with dwarves. And these dwarves worked in the mines beneath the surface of the earth and swore revenge at the up-worlders.

NARRATOR 1. Curse you, up-worlders!

DWARF 1. And one day they came home to find a beautiful girl sleeping in their bed.

NARRATOR 1. Hey look! A giant hottie!

DWARF 2. She's huge! She's going to eat me! Run for it!

(NARRATOR 1 holds up a hand.)

NARRATOR 1. Hold on, Dwarf Number Two. I'm tired of running. I'm tired of being a supporting character. This is my time. You see, I happen to be quite brilliant and I know for a fact that this giant hottie has fallen under a curse to sleep for a hundred years.

DWARF 2. I thought that was the Sleeping Beauty story.

NARRATOR 1. From my perspective, they all look the same. And the only way for this giant hottie to wake up is to receive a kiss from her true love. Me.

DWARF 2. Um . . . so you're going to kiss her without getting active consent?

NARRATOR 1. What are you doing?

DWARF 2. Just preparing my police report.

NARRATOR 1. Fine.

(NARRATOR 1 raps on something.)

NARRATOR 1. HEY. GIANT HOTTIE. IS IT COOL IF I KISS YOU TO WAKE YOU UP FROM YOUR COMA?

(NARRATOR 1 listens.)

(Then NARRATOR 1 *makes a little* SNOW WHITE *voice and says:)*

NARRATOR 1. Sure Dwarf One I would like that.

DWARF 2. That was you!

NARRATOR 1. Well how am I supposed to—?

DWARF 2. What if you did an air hug from a six foot distance?

NARRATOR 1. Fine.

(She backs up and air hugs SNOW WHITE. SNOW WHITE *wakes up.)*

SNOW WHITE. *(Waking up:)* Ah!

DWARF 1. It was love at first sight.

SNOW WHITE. Oh you're not what I expected.

NARRATOR 1. I'm better, baby. I am the mighty dwarf Slappy and I have rescued you from the evil curse that was—

SNOW WHITE. *(Overlapping:)* I was just tired, I wasn't under a curse—

NARRATOR 1. *(Overlapping:)* Forcing you to sleep for a hundred years. I am your true love.

(SNOW WHITE raises her hand.)

SNOW WHITE. Um.

DWARF 1. This is where you break into song.

SNOW WHITE. I don't know the words.

DWARF 1. That's okay— I wrote them down for you.

(DWARF 1 hands a sheet of paper to SNOW WHITE.*)*

(SNOW WHITE takes the sheet and looks at it.)

SNOW WHITE. This says I cook dinner and clean the house and leave the thinking to my husband.

DWARF 1. It's a perfect marriage.

SNOW WHITE. This is disgusting! I'm a modern woman!

DWARF 1. Well you're not going to live happily ever after then!

SNOW WHITE. I'm going to tell the story my way!

(She throws down the lyrics.)

(DWARF 2 and WITCH 2 enter.)

WITCH 2. Are y'all gonna need me any time soon?

SNOW WHITE. Yes. We are starting over right now. Once upon a time there was a beautiful girl.

(The actors look around. SNOW WHITE points at DWARF 2.)

(WITCH 2 exits, annoyed.)

SNOW WHITE. You're going to be Snow White this time.

(Author's note: Whatever the double-casting, it is imperative that DWARF 2 be played by a male-presenting actor.)

DWARF 2. ABOUT DANG TIME! YES!

(DWARF 2 grabs a stash of clothing. He has ALL of the Snow White stuff. Dress – tiara – wig – gloves – roses. He talks while he's putting on the dress and everything.)

DWARF 2. I've just been waiting for my chance but I will ROCK THIS. Oh yeah. It's my time. It's all coming true just like I dreamed. You can do this, *[Dwarf 2 actor's real name].*
Time for this diamond to shine.

(DWARF 2 prepares mentally, perhaps stretches, perhaps takes out a mirror to apply a beauty mark.)

DWARF 2. Showtime.

NARRATOR 1. All right then.

SNOW WHITE. She was the most beautiful girl in the entire kingdom.

(DWARF 2 struts up and down, as if he's on a runway.)

DWARF 2. You know it!

SNOW WHITE. But her stepmother was jealous.

(WITCH 2 returns as DWARF 2 struts.)

WITCH 2. Snow White.

DWARF 2. Stepmother.

WITCH 2. Is that a zit I see on your face?

DWARF 2. You'd like that, wouldn't you?

WITCH 2. I do believe you're skipping your exercise routine.

DWARF 2. Not on your life, sister. These curves are tight and streamlined like a racing yacht owned by a hip-hop mogul.

WITCH 2. I think you might need to tweeze your eyebrows. They're looking . . . puffy.

DWARF 2. No, they are fierce like a chained tiger with ghost peppers stuffed up his—

SNOW WHITE. *(Cutting him off:)* Moving on. And the wicked stepmother went to her room and gazed into her magic mirror.

(DWARF 1 *becomes the magic mirror.*)

WITCH 2. Mirror, mirror, on the wall. Who's the fairest of them all?

DWARF 1. *(As the mirror, a drawn-out ghostly voice:)* Well it's certainly not you.

WITCH 2. Curses!

DWARF 1. *(As the mirror:)* Hey that's a good idea. You should try that.

SNOW WHITE. Meanwhile, Snow White was only becoming more fierce.

(DWARF 2 *continues to strut.*)

DWARF 2. Work it. Work it.

SNOW WHITE. And just then—

(WITCH 2 *faces* DWARF 2.)

It was her stepmother.

WITCH 2. Stepmother.

DWARF 2. Snow White.

(They look confused. SNOW WHITE *gestures that they have it reversed.)*

WITCH 2. Snow White.

DWARF 2. Stepmother.

WITCH 2. I'm afraid it's over for you, Snow White. For I have a lot of money and have been though a lot of plastic surgery in Hollywood. Now, I am more beautiful than even you.

DWARF 2. Unlikely. BEGIN.

(DWARF 1 *starts some thrilling runway music.*)

(DWARF 2 *and* WITCH 2 *strut back and forth, throwing fierce looks at each other.*)

(NARRATOR 1 *becomes* PRINCE 2 *and enters. [Whoever plays* PRINCE 2 *should be female-presenting.])*

PRINCE 2. Yaaas Queen! Slay!

DWARF 1. Enough!

(They stop.)

DWARF 1. Snow White is still the fiercest.

WITCH 2. Dang it! Well, how about an apple as a peace offering?

DWARF 2. How 'bout I take you out with my martial arts skills?

WITCH 2. Oh it's on!

PRINCE 2. Not to interrupt but I was just in the neighborhood looking for a girl in a coma to make out with and—whoa! Chickfight!

(DWARF 2 and WITCH 2 circle each other.)

SNOW WHITE. And it was a glorious battle.

WITCH 2. *Expelliarmus!*

DWARF 2. *Expelliarmus* yourself!

(They start slap-fighting. It's ridiculous.)

PRINCE 2. Go Snow White!

SNOW WHITE. A titanic struggle of good and evil. Purity versus corruption.

(DWARF 2 pokes WITCH 2 in the eyes, 3 Stooges-style. WITCH 2 throws stuff at DWARF 2.)

SNOW WHITE. Until finally.

WITCH 2. I shall transform myself into a black dragon! Ah ha ha ha!

(Pause.)

SNOW WHITE. No that was in the Sleeping Beauty movie.

WITCH 2. I thought we were doing Sleeping Beauty.

SNOW WHITE. No this is Snow White.

(DWARF 2 takes a sword and stabs her.)

DWARF 2. Eat this, witch!

WITCH 2. Ah! I'm melting! Actually I'm . . . bleeding! Aaaaaah.

(WITCH 2 dies.)

PRINCE 2. That was so hot.

DWARF 2. Like somebody else I know, Prince.

PRINCE 2. You're very forward.

DWARF 2. I'm a modern woman. Come on, let's get married.

(DWARF 1 returns.)

SNOW WHITE. And just then.

DWARF 1. Hi ho. Hi ho.

DWARF 2. What'd you just call me?

DWARF 1. Um. Nothing. Look, I'm living with a bunch of other dwarves—

DWARF 2. I've heard enough! You are lucky enough to become my servants. Come with me.

SNOW WHITE. And they all lived happily ever after and avoided traditional gender roles. And the seven little dwarves cooked for them, cleaned the house, and did all that other junk that Snow White was supposed to do in the story. The end.

(NARRATOR 1 and NARRATOR 2 return.)

NARRATOR 1. That was enlightened.

SNOW WHITE. Thank you.

(She exits.)

NARRATOR 2. But the witch was not dead.

WITCH 2. It's just a flesh wound!

NARRATOR 1. Stop it. We're doing this without any Monty Python references.

WITCH 2. 'Tis but a scratch.

NARRATOR 1. I said stop it!

NARRATOR 2. Anyway, the witch felt bad and built a house made of candy and decided to eat children instead.

WITCH 2. There aren't many career options for me.

(She exits.)

NARRATOR 1. But the true secret origin here is of Dwarf Number Two.

NARRATOR 2. Which brings us to the darkest, most disturbing fairy tale ever told: Faithful Johannes.

(JOHANNES enters. He's all smiles. Very, very happy.)

NARRATOR 1. Never heard of it.

NARRATOR 2. There's a reason for that. Welcome to Faithful Johannes—the original psychological thriller.

(Lights change on JOHANNES in a creepy fashion. Perhaps a red light? He's no longer all smiles. He looks terrified.)

(NARRATOR 1 *changes into the* QUEEN.)

(KING *enters.*)

NARRATOR 2. Once upon a time there was a noble servant, Faithful Johannes, who served his king faithfully, as you might glean from his name.

KING. Hey everybody! Check out my servant, Faithful Johannes!

JOHANNES. You're too kind, your majesty.

KING. He's the best! All your other servants are GARBAGE. Faithful Johannes would do anything for me! Eat a bug. Do it.

JOHANNES. Of course, sire.

(*JOHANNES eats a bug and smiles afterwards.*)

KING. HE LOVES IT. All your other servants are LOSERS. Nobody like Faithful Johannes here! Slap yourself in the face for me.

(*JOHANNES slaps himself in the face. Smiles afterwards.*)

AMAZING. All right, I'm goin' to bed. In conclusion: Faithful Johannes is the best, and all other servants are STUPID.

(KING *exits.*)

NARRATOR 2. Johannes loved his life.

JOHANNES. This is great. Nothing like eating bugs and slapping myself in the face for my King.

(*He sighs and tries to keep it together.*)

NARRATOR 2. But one night he was visited . . .

(RAVEN *enters [or* NARRATOR 2 *transforms into* RAVEN]. RAVEN *is dressed in a black trenchcoat or looks suitably sketchy.*)

NARRATOR 2. By a talking raven.

RAVEN. Hey Pssst. Yo Johannes.

JOHANNES. Who's that?

RAVEN. C'mere. I got something to tell you.

JOHANNES. Are you a talking raven?

RAVEN. Yeah. Shaddup. I got news for you.

JOHANNES. What is it?

RAVEN. There's about to be three attempts on the King's life. You wanna stop it? You listen to me.

JOHANNES. Oh.

RAVEN. But you breathe a word of this, you tell anybody you heard it from me, I'll turn you to stone.

JOHANNES. You can do that?

RAVEN. I can do anything I want. I'm a talking raven. You got it? *(Harsh whisper:)* Don't tell nobody nothing.

JOHANNES. O-okay.

RAVEN. First up: You didn't hear this from me, but there's a magic horse—

JOHANNES. A magic horse?

RAVEN. Shhhhh! And the King's gonna think he's pretty sweet, but if he gets on that horse, the horse is gonna fly into the air and the King's gonna fall from about two thousand feet. Splat. So here's what you're gonna do: You're gonna take this gun, and you're gonna shoot that horse in the face.

> (RAVEN *produces a toy gun.*)

JOHANNES. But I'm in a fairy tale, I didn't even know we had guns.

RAVEN. You do now. You understand me? You shoot that horse, or the King is dead meat. And I'll be watching you.

> (RAVEN *points towards* JOHANNES' *eyes.*)

Ca-CAW!

> (JOHANNES *freaks out.* RAVEN *flies off.*)

NARRATOR 2. The next day.

> (KING *returns.*)

KING. Well my Faithful Johannes let's go for a lovely stroll!

> (JOHANNES *freaks out and puts the gun behind his back.*)

JOHANNES. *(Twitchy and nervous:)* Of course sire.

KING. Something the matter?

JOHANNES. Not at all! I'm—fine.

> (JOHANNES *looks in all directions, paranoid. Spins. Looks behind him.*)

> (PLINKIE PLIE, *an adorably cute pink flying horse, enters.*)

KING. Hey look at that!

> (PLINKIE PLIE *waves coquettishly.*)

PLINKIE PLIE. Oh hi there! My name's Plinkie Pie! I'm a magical—

(*BLAM!*)

(JOHANNES *stands, shaking, gun in hand, staring wide-eyed.*)

PLINKIE PLIE. Aaaaaah. I'm dying! Tell my friends they were magic . . .

(PLINKIE PLIE *dies.*)

KING. WHAT THE HECK?

JOHANNES. I didn't like the look of that horse, sire.

KING. THAT WAS AN ADORABLE HORSE. Why would you do that?!

JOHANNES. Um . . . stress at home. Sorry.

KING. Man. You got problems.

(KING *exits.*)

NARRATOR 2. Later that night.

(RAVEN *enters behind* JOHANNES.)

(JOHANNES *stands, shaking, eyes wide.*)

RAVEN. Psst. Yo Johannes. C'mere.

JOHANNES. Ah! Stay away from me! I can't do this!

RAVEN. Attempt number two is comin' tomorrow. At the King's wedding rehearsal.

JOHANNES. I don't want to hear it!

RAVEN. It's gotta be you, Johannes. The King's wedding shirt is cursed. If he puts it on, he'll burn to death.

JOHANNES. I don't believe you! That horse was innocent! And I killed her! I . . . killed . . . her . . .

RAVEN. All you need to do is stop the king from taking the shirt, and tear it up in front of him. That's all you gotta do. But remember— you don't say nothing to nobody, or I'll turn you to stone.

JOHANNES. How do I know you're telling the truth?!

RAVEN. You don't. (RAVEN *chuckles.*) Ca-CAW!

(JOHANNES *jumps.*)

(KING *and* QUEEN *enter as the* RAVEN *flies off.*)

(JOHANNES *watches, freaking out, twitching.*)

QUEEN. Welcome friends. It's so nice to see all of you mostly recovered from the plague. And I'm here to tell you I love this big guy. Come here, ya big galoot. This is a day of celebration. 'Cause I love you, honey bear.

KING. I love you more, honey bear!

QUEEN. Even our nicknames are cute! This is the happiest day of my life! And—as a little present—I made you something.

(She reaches down and takes out a t-shirt.)

I sewed this myself! It's the only thing I've ever done myself. And I made it . . . for you.

KING. Oh it's—

(JOHANNES lunges and snatches it out of the QUEEN's hand.)

JOHANNES. AHHHHHHHHHHH!

(He tries to rip it up, can't—grabs some scissors and tears holes in it. He throws it on the ground and stomps on it again and again.)

JOHANNES. I HATE THIS SHIRT! I HATE IT!

(Pause. He stops. Everyone is looking at him.)

KING. Um . . . WHAT. THE. HECK.

JOHANNES. It's not your color, sire. It is an affront against fashion.

(QUEEN bursts into tears.)

KING. Oh honey bear!

QUEEN. I'm never going to try again!

(She sobs. Runs off.)

KING. I gotta deal with this. Johannes? Not. Cool.

(He follows her off.)

NARRATOR 2. That night.

(JOHANNES looks around, freaking out.)

JOHANNES. I don't want to hear from any talking birds tonight!

(RAVEN enters.)

No! No! Get out!

RAVEN. Yo Johannes. You did good, kid.

JOHANNES. Everyone thinks I'm crazy!

RAVEN. Tomorrow, the Queen is gonna die.

JOHANNES. Stop it!

RAVEN. She's gonna be poisoned. And the only way to stop it is for you . . . to suck three drops out of blood out of the queen's breast.

JOHANNES. WHA-A-A-A-T?

RAVEN. Upper chest region.

JOHANNES. STILL.

RAVEN. Fine. Don't do it. She'll die. No difference to me. Remember—don't tell nobody nothing.

JOHANNES. I'm not doing it! You can't make me!

RAVEN. Ca-CAW!

> *(RAVEN flies off.)*
>
> *(JOHANNES paces nervously.)*
>
> *(KING and QUEEN enter. Both have glasses of wine.)*

QUEEN. Okay I had a rough night remembering that shirt, but I'm feeling a little better. Obviously, it was traumatic for everyone and I'm going to be okay with fifteen or twenty years of therapy. But today is not about the terrible trauma of yesterday, today is about putting a happy face on . . . and . . . and . . . urk . . .

> *(She falls over.)*
>
> *(It's important she falls over behind something so that we can't see her body.)*

KING 2. Oh no! Are you all right, Honey Bear? Say something! Is there a doctor in the house?

> *(JOHANNES just stares.)*

Can anyone save the Queen's life? Anyone at all?

> *(JOHANNES just stares.)*

Oh no this is terrible! Someone do something! If only someone could save her!

> *(JOHANNES drops down where the QUEEN has fallen [so that the audience can't see him].)*
>
> *(KING watches in horror.)*

KING 2. WHOA. WHAT. THE. HECK.

> *(QUEEN and JOHANNES get back up.)*

QUEEN. Thanks. I feel better.

KING. DUDE! JOHANNES. EXPLAIN YOURSELF.

JOHANNES. Um . . .

KING. THAT IS IT. You are sentenced to death for being a jerk! Where's my guillotine?

JOHANNES. Wait! I always served you faithfully, sire! But there was a talking raven who was threatening me and telling me—urk . . .

NARRATOR 2. And just then, Johannes turned into a statue. Because when a magic raven says stuff to you, you better listen.

NARRATOR 1. Okay, that was mildly traumatic but not super traumatic —

NARRATOR 2. Ten years passed. And every day the King would stare at the statue of Faithful Johannes and sigh . . .

QUEEN. Are you coming up to bed?

KING 2. Hold on. I'm gonna spend some more time with this statue. He was such a good servant.

QUEEN. All right I'm going to sleep.

(KING *mimes stroking the statue.*)

KING. If only there was some way to bring you back. No one eats bugs or slaps themselves in the face for me any more.

NARRATOR 2. And just then a ghostly voice emanated from the statue . . .

JOHANNES. Ooooooohhhhh . . . there is one way . . . To . . . bring me back . . .

KING 2. What is it?! I'll do anything!

JOHANNES. Take what you love most in the world . . .

KING 2. That would be my two boys. I love my two boys so much.

(He holds up two puppets.)

Daddy loves you.

(As the puppets:)

"I love you, Papa."
"You're the best, Daddy."

JOHANNES. Chop off their heads and smear their blood on me . . .

KING. Done!

(He rips off the puppets' heads — [or throws them down and stomps on them.])

(Then pulls out two headless puppets with red on their necks and mimes smearing their blood on the statue.)

(JOHANNES comes back to life.)

JOHANNES. Ohhh. I feel so much better!

KING. You're alive! Air hug!

(They air hug.)

(They dance and dance, high-five each other.)

(KING and JOHANNES dance off, hand-in-hand.)

NARRATOR 2. And the King and Johannes lived happily ever after. The end.

(NARRATOR 1 enters, stunned.)

NARRATOR 1. What did I just watch?

NARRATOR 2. That's the fairy tale. Right there.

NARRATOR 1. He kills his children to bring back his servant?

NARRATOR 2. A good servant is really hard to find. You can always make more kids. Okay fine— Johannes resurrects the kids later because he's got superpowers, and then one of those kids runs away from home, becomes a dwarf, and lives in the mines.

NARRATOR 1. Wow. That is messedup.

NARRATOR 2. Yup.

NARRATOR 2. Well, I think we're running out of time.

NARRATOR 1. But we didn't get to The Frog Prince, or Little Red Riding Hood, or the Devil's Grandmother.

NARRATOR 2. We've done the important ones though.

(CINDERELLA enters.)

CINDERELLA. Ahem.

NARRATOR 2. What?

CINDERELLA. Aren't you forgetting something?

NARRATOR 2. Oh.

CINDERELLA. Yeah.

NARRATOR 1. All right one last one. Once upon a time—

CINDERELLA. Thank you.

(She does some deep breathing exercises.)

NARRATOR 2. There was a little orphan girl.

(CINDERELLA overacts.)

CINDERELLA. Oh I am orphaned! Oh I am sad!

(ACTOR enters as CINDERELLA whimpers piteously.)

ACTOR. Can we pause here for a second?

CINDERELLA. Oh how sad I am!

ACTOR. Just hold on.

NARRATOR 1. What is it?

ACTOR. There was like some really bad beef in the catering

CINDERELLA. Oh the catering is bad!

ACTOR. So like everybody is throwing up back here.

NARRATOR 1. Excuse me.

(NARRATOR 1 runs off.)

ACTOR. So we don't have enough actors to do this one.

(CINDERELLA stops acting.)

CINDERELLA. What?

NARRATOR 2. Well I guess we can skip it then.

CINDERELLA. NO WE ARE NOT SKIPPING IT.

NARRATOR 2. How many actors do we have left?

ACTOR. Um . . . me.

CINDERELLA. Now you listen to me you little reject from Nickelodeon—this is my chance to be a star, got it? There are important people watching—probably—and I'm getting an HBO series out of this, got it?

ACTOR. Well, I—

CINDERELLA. GOT IT? OR I WILL TEAR OUT YOUR TINY HEART.

ACTOR. Yes, ma'am.

CINDERELLA. Thank you.

(CINDERELLA immediately goes back to acting sad.)

Oh how sad. Life. So sad.

NARRATOR 2. Okay, so, her mother died and her father remarried—

CINDERELLA. Mother? Where are you Mother? Are you dead?

NARRATOR 2. And the woman he married was beautiful of face but black of heart.

CINDERELLA. I shall spread these cinders upon myself to keep me warm. Ah, they're hot! Ow!

NARRATOR 2. So they called her Cinderella. Now, Cinderella's stepmother had two daughters, both equally beautiful—

CINDERELLA. I'm sorry. You're wrong. I'm the pretty one. They're quite hideous.

NARRATOR 2. Says here they're beautiful too.

CINDERELLA. I think I know my story, thank you.

(*She returns to the floor.*)

Oh they are so mean to me. I shall now cry like I do every night.

(*She cries sadly.*)

(*From this point on,* ACTOR *uses different props or wigs to signify different characters. These should be increasingly ridiculous, starting with wigs for the Wicked Stepsisters and moving on to weirder and weirder things—rave hats, oversize sunglasses, stuffed animals, fake beards, Mickey Mouse ears—this should be a completely eclectic bunch of random stuff.*)

(*NOTE: If possible, all different characters should have different voices or accents.*)

NARRATOR 2. Just then her two wicked stepsisters entered.

(ACTOR *grabs two wigs and swings open the door to their room.*)

ACTOR. (*As Wicked Stepsister 1:*) Look what the cat dragged in.

(*Switches wigs.*)

(*As Wicked Stepsister 2:*) Does it smell in here, or is it just her?

(*Switches wigs.*)

(*As Wicked Stepsister 1:*) Oh that was a good one, Jiselle.

(*Switches wigs.*)

(*As Wicked Stepsister 2:*) Thought you'd like it.

(*Switches wigs.*)

(*As Wicked Stepsister 1:*) Oh Cinderella. I need to get ready for the ball—

CINDERELLA. What ball?

ACTOR. *(As Wicked Stepsister 1:)* The ball being thrown by Prince Charming.

(Switches wigs.)

(As Wicked Stepsister 2:) He's so charming. When I see him I just want to grab his little tights-wearing bottom and squeeze.

CINDERELLA. May I attend the ball?

ACTOR. *(As Wicked Stepsister 2:)* Um . . . No?

(Switches wigs.)

(As Wicked Stepsister 1:) You're going to make us pretty.

(Switches wigs.)

(As Wicked Stepsister 2:) Make me prettier than her. I need Charming. I need him. Now.

CINDERELLA. I suppose. I'm going to need a lot of makeup.

NARRATOR 2. Cinderella dressed both sisters for the ball.

ACTOR. *(Checking himself out)*

(As Wicked Stepsister 1:) I'm so hot.

(Switches wigs, checks himself out even more.)

(As Wicked Stepsister 2:) I'm gorgeous. Rarrrr.

(ACTOR exits with both wigs.)

CINDERELLA. *(Overacting:)* Life. So unfair. Why am I just a servant? Why, Mama? Why?

(She cries even more piteously.)

NARRATOR 2. But just then, her wicked stepmother entered.

(ACTOR enters, in a more ridiculous wig.)

ACTOR. *(As Wicked Stepmother:)* Why Cinderella, what seems to be the trouble?

CINDERELLA. I can't go to the ball! I am so sad!

ACTOR. *(As Wicked Stepmother:)* Come here and sit on your step-mother's lap.

(CINDERELLA eyes her suspiciously.)

CINDERELLA. That's weird.

ACTOR. *(As Wicked Stepmother:)* Get over it.

(She sits gingerly on her stepmother's lap.)

ACTOR. *(As Wicked Stepmother:)*Would you like to go to the ball with us?

NARRATOR 2. Just then, one of Cinderella's stepsisters, Jiselle, entered through the door.

(ACTOR looks angrily at NARRATOR, drops CINDERELLA off their lap, runs off and returns in a different wig.)

ACTOR. *(As Wicked Stepsister 2:)* Mother aren't you coming?

(ACTOR runs up to where the Stepmother was, switches wig, puts CINDERELLA back on their lap.)

ACTOR. *(As Wicked Stepmother:)* In a moment dear, run along.

(He dumps Cinderella, runs back to the door, switches wigs.)

(As Wicked Stepsister 2:) Thank you I will.

NARRATOR 2. And just then, from the other side of the room, Cinderella's other Wicked Stepsister entered.

(The ACTOR gives NARRATOR 2 an evil look and rushes to the other side of the stage, switching wigs as they go.)

ACTOR. *(As Wicked Stepsister 1:)* I really need to be going.

(Runs back to the door, switches wigs.)

(As Wicked Stepsister 2:) You do that. Witch.

(Runs back to the other side of the room, switches wigs.)

(As Wicked Stepsister 1:) What did you just call me?

(Runs back to the door, switches wigs.)

(As Wicked Stepsister 2:) You heard what I said. Witch.

(Runs back to the other side of the room, switches wigs.)

(As Wicked Stepsister 1:) Oh no you didn't!

(Switches wigs, runs and puts Cinderella on their lap.)

ACTOR. *(As Wicked Stepmother:)* Girls, please! You're both pretty. You're both going to the ball. You both need to exit right now without saying anything else.

NARRATOR 2. And so . . . they left.

ACTOR. *(As Wicked Stepmother:)* Thank you. Now Cinderella, I am a fair wicked stepmother, so . . . I am going to empty an entire dish of lentils into the fireplace, and once you have picked them all out you may go to the ball with us.

NARRATOR 2. And with that, she dumped a dish of lentils into the fireplace like she said she was going to do.

(ACTOR *exits.*)

CINDERELLA. Oh, the humanity! Oh Gods! Why must I always be punished!?

NARRATOR 2. I mean, it's just a couple of lentils, that doesn't seem all that hard to—

CINDERELLA. I will never go! Never! I am cursed! But what's that? What could it be?

(*She pops up to listen.*)

My fairy—

NARRATOR 2. It was a swarm of birds.

(ACTOR *enters, raising their hand.*)

ACTOR. Question: Do I have to play each individual bird or can I be collectively, The Birds?

NARRATOR 2. I guess you can be a collective group of birds.

ACTOR. You have no idea how much that means to me.

(ACTOR *picks up a feather boa and runs around as the birds.*)

(*As the birds:*) Tweet! Tweet tweet! Tweet tweet tweet!

CINDERELLA. Oh look, birds! They're so beautiful! Come, my little feathered friends, come and peck these lentils out of the fireplace.

(ACTOR *mimes pecking.*)

ACTOR. (*As the birds:*) Peck peck peck peck peck! Peck peck peck!

CINDERELLA. Oh I am truly blessed! Thank you birds! Fly, fly to freedom!

(ACTOR *one throws the boa or feathers into the air and runs out, grabbing a wig.*)

ACTOR. (*As Wicked Stepmother:*) We're off to the ball!

CINDERELLA. Look, Wicked Stepmother! I have removed all of the lentils.

ACTOR. (*As Wicked Stepmother:*) Really?

(*She moves forward to examine the fireplace.*)

(*As Wicked Stepmother:*) Well ain't that a kick in the pants.

CINDERELLA. So I will be accompanying you to the ball! Oh how I love balls! *

(She stops, looks mortified.)

(* This line may be cut.)

ACTOR. *(As Wicked Stepmother:)* Frankly, I don't think you're good enough for balls. Besides, you've got nothing to wear. Too bad. Have to be going.

(Runs out, returns in a wig.)

(As Wicked Stepsister 1:) Ha ha!

(Runs out, switches wigs, returns.)

(As Wicked Stepsister 2:) Loser!

CINDERELLA. How can life be so cruel! WHY?!!!! What's that? My fairy—

NARRATOR 2. It was another swarm of birds, carrying a dress.

(ACTOR returns with boa or feather, carrying a dress.)

ACTOR. *(As the birds:)* Tweet tweet! Tweet tweet!

CINDERELLA. What a lovely dress. Thank you, swarm of birds.

ACTOR. *(As the birds:)* Tweet tweet tweet!

CINDERELLA. So who's going to do my hair? Um . . . what a surprise, a fairy godmother.

(Pause.)

Isn't this where she sorta comes in and does her magic thing?

NARRATOR 2. Nope.

CINDERELLA. What?

NARRATOR 2. We're going by the original. There's no fairy godmother. Just a lot of birds.

ACTOR. *(As the birds:)* Tweet tweet tweet.

CINDERELLA. Well I can't do this without a fairy godmother! Who's going to turn the pumpkin into a coach?

NARRATOR 2. You walk there.

CINDERELLA. What?! This is ridiculous! I'm Cinderella! I have a fairy godmother, and a coach made out of a pumpkin and a bunch of mice turned into coachmen! Oh so there's no mice either is there! Next thing you know there won't even be a glass slipper—

(NARRATOR 2 shakes his head.)

THERE'S NO GLASS SLIPPER!? Well, then I don't even know how this story goes! Maybe I just get beheaded at the end? I JUST GET BEHEADED AT THE END?!!

NARRATOR 2. Maybe. I don't know. I haven't read to the end yet.

CINDERELLA. Ahhhhh! I QUIT!

(She pulls out her cell-phone.)

Yeah this is Cindy. I don't know what they're doing any more. They're going by the original fairy tale and there's no mice coachmen and I can't work like this. I DON'T KNOW WHY THERE'S NO MICE COACHMEN!!! I can't do this!

(She exits in a huff.)

(It's just ACTOR and NARRATOR 2 now.)

NARRATOR 2. Well, guess somebody's not living happily ever after is she? All right then, let's continue with our story.

ACTOR. Um . . . we can't continue. There's no Cinderella.

NARRATOR 2. Sure there is.

(NARRATOR 2 stares at ACTOR.)

Put on the dress, *[name]* .

(ACTOR stares at NARRATOR 2, then slowly, unhappily, puts on the dress.)

NARRATOR 2. So Cinderella had her dress. And she felt very pretty.

ACTOR. *(As Cinderella:)* I feel very pretty. Thank you birds.

(Grabs the feather or boa.)

(As the birds:) Tweet tweet tweet tweet!

(Drops the feather.)

(As Cinderella:) Now I shall walk to the ball.

(He walks around the room.)

NARRATOR 2. And just then Cinderella's Wicked Stepmother and two wicked stepsisters arrived.

(ACTOR runs out, returns with three more wigs.)

ACTOR. *(As Wicked Stepmother:)* Cinderella!

(Switches wigs.)

ACTOR. *(As Wicked Stepsister 1:)* What are you doing here?

(Switches wigs.)

(As Wicked Stepsister 2:) We hate you!

(Drops all the wigs, gets back into the Cinderella dress.)

(As Cinderella:) I have a dress and I'm going to the ball because the birds brought it to me!

NARRATOR 2. And it was a wonderful ball, a huge ball. And everyone started dancing. Unfortunately, the Wicked Stepmother only knew how to cha-cha, one stepsister was doing a waltz, and the other one was twerking.

(ACTOR has stopped, exhausted, and is staring at NARRATOR 2.)

Do it.

(ACTOR spits on the floor and tries it.)

ACTOR. *(As Wicked Stepmother, doing the cha-cha:)* You should go dance with the Prince.

(Switches wigs, starts waltzing.)

(As Wicked Stepsister 1:) He's so dreamy.

(Switches wigs, starts twerking.)

(As Wicked Stepsister 2:) YES.

(ACTOR runs out, returns wearing a hat or giant glasses and blowing an imaginary horn.)

(As Herald:) Dun de dun dun! His royal highness the Prince!

(Goes out the door, drops the hat or glasses, and puts on a crown.)

(As Prince Charming, with British accent:) 'Ello there. We're having a nice time, are we? Blimey. Who's that minx, she's gorgeous!

(Runs, gets into the Cinderella dress.)

(As Cinderella:) My name's not important.

(Switches back to Prince.)

(As Prince Charming:) Right-o. Come here and give us a taste, love.

(Switches back to Cinderella— They dance back and forth.)

(As Cinderella:) Oh Prince. You're embarrassing me.

(Switches back to Prince.)

(As Prince Charming:) Blimey. You skin's as supple as a baby's bottom!

(Back to Cinderella.)

ACTOR. *(As Cinderella:)* I moisturize.

> *(Back to Prince Charming.)*

(As Prince Charming:) I'd like to pour hot sauce on you and roast you over an open pit till you're brown and tender.

> *(Back to Cinderella.)*

(As Cinderella:) I'd like that.

> *(ACTOR makes out with himself.)*

NARRATOR 2. All right, this is getting weird. I have to say I'm pretty impressed, though. Maybe he should get the HBO special.

> *(CINDERELLA [the real one] returns.)*

CINDERELLA. What HBO special?

> *(ACTOR keeps going. CINDERELLA watches the action, annoyed.)*

ACTOR. *(As Cinderella:)* I have to leave, Prince.

> *(Back to Prince Charming.)*

(As Prince Charming:) What's your name, love?

> *(Back to Cinderella, running away.)*

(As Cinderella:) It would spoil everything if you knew my name!

CINDERELLA. Just tell him your name, sheesh.

> *(ACTOR comes back and becomes the Prince again. Sinks to his knees.)*

ACTOR. *(As Prince Charming:)* No! I could've loved you! Especially because you were attractive!

CINDERELLA. Isn't she supposed to drop a slipper or something?

NARRATOR 2. Cinderella loses a slipper on her third trip to the Prince's ball. He keeps throwing more balls, and she keeps freaking out, until finally the Prince smears pitch on the steps of the palace, and then her shoe sticks, her golden shoe by the way—

CINDERELLA. Golden shoe?

NARRATOR 2. And he comes looking for the foot that fits the golden shoe.

CINDERELLA. Huh. That does sound more comfortable than glass.

> *(ACTOR raises his hand.)*

ACTOR. Can we skip to that part please? I'm going to die.

CINDERELLA. Maybe you should put a little effort into this.

ACTOR. Why don't you play your own part?

CINDERELLA. You're doing fine, sweetie. I'll just watch.

NARRATOR 2. Fine. A little of this, a little of that, the Prince stops by with a shoe looking for a girl who fits it.

(ACTOR takes a deep breath, then grabs the Prince's clothes and holds up a tennis shoe.)

ACTOR. *(As Prince Charming:)* 'Ello then. Any of you darlings lost a shoe?

(He grabs a wig.)

(As Wicked Stepsister 1:) Oh I did. I did. Let me see that!

(Hands the shoe to himself.)

(As Wicked Stepsister 1:) Hold on one minute. Do you mind if I try this on in the bathroom? I'm shy.

(Switches back to the Prince.)

(As Prince Charming:) Take all the time you like, love.

(Puts the wig back on.)

(As Wicked Stepsister 1:) Excellent.

(ACTOR moves off to the side.)

NARRATOR 2. And of course her foot was too big, so she chopped off her big toe.

ACTOR. *(As Wicked Stepsister 1, a blood-curdling scream, offstage:)* Aarrrrrrrrrrrrrrrrrrrrgghghghghg!

(Comes back, becomes Prince.)

(As Prince Charming:) Say, you all right in there?

(Leaves again.)

(As Wicked Stepsister 1:) Aarrrrhghghghghg.

(ACTOR hops in on one foot, then limps over.)

(As Wicked Stepsister 1:) It . . . fits . . . fine. I . . . love . . . you.

(Switches back to being the Prince.)

(As Prince Charming:) Bangers and mash! Let's go get married then. 'Op into me carriage.

(ACTOR mime sitting down, holding foot.)

(As Wicked Stepsister 1:) It's . . . nice . . . gargggghhhh.

(Switches back to the Prince.)

ACTOR. *(As Prince Charming:)* Say, what's all this then? There's blood everywhere.

(Puts wig back on.)

(As Wicked Stepsister 1:) I popped a zit. On my foot.

(Back to Prince.)

(As Prince Charming:) You chopped off your toe, you did! Out of my carriage you!

NARRATOR 2. So the Wicked Stepsister went back home and the Prince returned to find Cinderella's other Wicked Stepsister.

(ACTOR switches into the other wig.)

ACTOR. *(As Wicked Stepsister 2:)* May I please try the shoe on in the bathroom so no one can watch what I'm doing?

(Switches back to the Prince.)

(AS PRInce Charming:) Of course, I'm not all that bright.

(ACTOR walks off with the shoe again.)

NARRATOR 2. And once she was in the bathroom, the shoe didn't feet either. So she did the only sensible thing and chopped off her heel.

ACTOR. *(Blood-curdling scream:)* *(As Wicked Stepsister 2:)* OHHHH! SWEET BEAUTIFUL BUNNIES! ARRRRGHGHGH!

(He runs back in, takes up the Prince's crown.)

(As Prince Charming:) All right in there?

(ACTOR switches wigs, limps in.)

(As Wicked Stepsister 2:) I'm . . . fine. Arrrrrgh. See . . . it fits.

(Switches back.)

(As Prince Charming:) All right then, let's get married. Jump in me carriage.

NARRATOR 2. But as they were riding . . .

ACTOR. *(As Prince Charming:)* Blimey! Is that blood on your foot?

(Puts on the wig.)

(As Wicked Stepsister 2:) I cut myself shaving. I have hairy feet. Like a hobbit.

(Switches.)

ACTOR. *(As Prince Charming:)* You cut off your heel!

    (Puts on the wig.)

(As Wicked Stepsister 2:) I did it for you!

NARRATOR 2. And so the Prince returned to the house for a third time.

ACTOR. *(As Prince Charming:)* 'Ello there. I realize several of the ladies in this here house have chopped off body parts to fit in this here shoe, but I was just wondering if anyone else fit in it. You see, I'm not very smart, but I make up for it by being very persistent. It makes me ideal to run the government.

    (He's about to switch again, but CINDERELLA *raises her hand.)*

CINDERELLA. I will try the shoe.

ACTOR. Oh thank goodness.

CINDERELLA. It fits!

ACTOR. *(As Prince Charming:)* It is you!

CINDERELLA. It is I!

NARRATOR 2. And they lived. Happily. Ever. After. As for the wicked stepsisters. The swarm of birds pecked out their eyes. Just for fun.

    (ACTOR grabs the feather exhaustedly.)

ACTOR. *(As the birds:)* Peck. Peck. Peck.

    (NARRATOR 1 returns.)

NARRATOR 1. However.

ACTOR. I don't think so.

    (ACTOR falls over, exhausted.)

NARRATOR 1. BUT -

NARRATOR 2. That's just the beginning.

NARRATOR 1. Exactly.

NARRATOR 2. I thought your had the beef?

NARRATOR 1. Oh, we were all fine. We just wanted to see if he could do it.

NARRATOR 2. That's not very nice.

NARRATOR 1. Eh. What can you do? Well, we're out of time—

NARRATOR 2. So it's time for the lightning round recap!

NARRATOR 1. It is?

NARRATOR 2. Of course. Otherwise no one would be able to follow the narrative. So what we're going to do to finish off the show is re-perform everything we've already done . . . in two minutes. Ready?

NARRATOR 1. I was born ready.

NARRATOR 2. All right then. And . . . GO!

NARRATOR 1. Cinderella got pregnant—

CINDERELLA. Heavens!

NARRATOR 1. After they were married.

CINDERELLA. Joyous day!

NARRATOR 2. And their daughter grew up to marry a guy with a great servant—

    (QUEEN runs in.)

QUEEN. I'm old now!

    (The KING runs in.)

KING. And I have a faithful servant!

JOHANNES. The bird told me to suck the poison out of— Ah I'm a statue!

KING. Oh no!

JOHANNES. Kill your children and I'll come back!

KING. Deal!

    (DWARF 1 runs in—)

DWARF 1. I've been resurrected but I'm a little peeved so I'm going to start my own dwarf village with six of my friends!

    (DWARF 2 runs in.)

DWARF 2. That's a great idea!

    (SNOW WHITE runs in.)

DWARF 1. Ah a giant hottie!

SNOW WHITE. Ah a dwarf!

DWARF 2. Little person!

DWARF 1. How 'bout you clean our house and tuck us in at night?

SNOW WHITE. You're not going to oppress me!

    (The WITCH runs in from the other direction.)